Lerner SPORTS

SPORTS

VIPs

MEET

SYDNEY McLAUGHLIN

MARGARET J. GOLDSTEIN

Lerner Publications ◆ Minneapolis

SPORTS THRILLS MEET RESEARCH SKILLS

Lerner SPORTS

Free Database Trial: **lernersports.com**

Copyright © 2023 by Lerner Publishing Group, Inc.

Lerner Publications Company
An imprint of Lerner Publishing Group, Inc.
241 First Avenue North
Minneapolis, MN 55401 USA

For reading levels and more information, look up this title at www.lernerbooks.com.

Main body text set in Aptifer Slab LT Pro. Typeface provided by Linotype AG.

Editor: Lauren Foley

Library of Congress Cataloging-in-Publication Data

Names: Goldstein, Margaret J., author.
Title: Meet Sydney McLaughlin / Margaret J. Goldstein.
Description: Minneapolis : Lerner Publications, 2023. | Series: Sports VIPs (Lerner sports) | Includes
    bibliographical references and index. | Audience: Ages 7–11 | Audience: Grades 2–3 | Summary: "At the Tokyo
    Olympics in 2021, Sydney McLaughlin scored two gold medals and broke the record for the fastest 400-meter
    hurdles time. Learn about her life as a track-and-field star"— Provided by publisher.
Identifiers: LCCN 2021051346 (print) | LCCN 2021051347 (ebook) | ISBN 9781728458212 (library binding) |
    ISBN 9781728463315 (paperback) | ISBN 9781728462295 (ebook)
Subjects: LCSH: McLaughlin, Sydney, 1999– —Juvenile literature. | Women track and field athletes—United
    States—Biography—Juvenile literature. | Women Olympic athletes—United States—Biography—Juvenile
    literature.
Classification: LCC GV697.M43 G65 2023 (print) | LCC GV697.M43 (ebook) | DDC 796.42092 [B]—dc23/eng/20211222

LC record available at https://lccn.loc.gov/2021051346
LC ebook record available at https://lccn.loc.gov/2021051347.gov/2021053235

Manufactured in the United States of America
1-50851-50188-2/2/2022

TABLE OF CONTENTS

>>>>>>>>>>>>>>>>>>>>>>>>

TICKET TO TOKYO

Sydney McLaughlin stood calmly on the track at Hayward Field in Eugene, Oregon, preparing for the women's 400-meter hurdles. It was the last day of the 2021 US Track and Field Olympic Trials. If the 21-year-old finished in the top three in this race, she'd make the US Olympic Team.

McLaughlin and seven other runners waited in their lanes for the race to begin. Each lane held 10 hurdles, evenly spaced along the 400-meter course. The runners would sprint down the track and leap over each hurdle.

FAST FACTS

DATE OF BIRTH: August 7, 1999

LEAGUE: USA Track and Field

PROFESSIONAL HIGHLIGHTS: Won gold medals in the 400-meter hurdles and the 4 x 400-meter relay at the 2021 Olympics; set a world record for 400-meter hurdles time; was the youngest member of the 2016 US Olympic Track Team

PERSONAL HIGHLIGHTS: Won the Gatorade National Player of the Year award twice; has endorsement deal with New Balance; got engaged to be married to former pro football player Andre Levrone Jr. in 2021

McLaughlin focuses as she clears a hurdle.

Dalilah Muhammad was in this race. She won a gold medal at the 2016 Olympic Games. At the 2019 World Championships, she finished the 400-meter hurdles in 52.16 seconds to set a world record. She was favored to win at the Olympic Trials too.

The opening gun sounded, and the women bolted. Muhammad quickly took the lead. But McLaughlin was right behind her. At the ninth hurdle, she caught up to Muhammad and surged ahead. Pouring it on over the final hurdle, she crossed the finish line in first place.

As McLaughlin cruised past the line, a big screen showed her winning time: 51.90 seconds. Jaws dropped all over the stadium. McLaughlin had smashed Muhammad's world record.

McLaughlin and Muhammad compete at the Olympic Trials in 2021.

When McLaughlin saw her record-breaking time, she covered her mouth in surprise. Muhammad hugged and congratulated her. The third-place finisher, Anna Cockrell, also celebrated. They were all going to the Olympics in Tokyo, Japan.

McLaughlin races ahead of Muhammad.

McLaughlin waves to the crowd after winning the 400-meter hurdles at the Olympic Trials.

McLaughlin was excited. She'd been to the Olympics in 2016 but had not won a medal. So she had another chance to race for the gold. She posted on Instagram the next day, "Congrats to everyone who made the team, as well as my awesome competitors!! Let's go represent the USA . . . the best way we know how!"

CHAPTER 1

RUNS IN THE FAMILY

Sydney McLaughlin was born into a family of runners on August 7, 1999, in New Brunswick, New Jersey. Her dad, Willie McLaughlin, ran track at Manhattan College in New York. He competed in the 400-meter race at the

1984 Olympic Trials but didn't make the team. Her mom, Mary Neumeister McLaughlin, ran track in high school and managed the Manhattan College track team. They had four children: Morgan, Taylor, Sydney, and Ryan.

McLaughlin's brother Taylor competes in a 400-meter hurdle event.

The family lived in Dunellen, New Jersey. Like their parents, all the kids ran track. Sydney ran her first competitive race at the age of six. It was a 100-meter sprint at a kids' event hosted by the Amateur Athletic Union (AAU). Her parents promised her a chocolate bar if she won. She finished with a huge lead over the other runners.

Like the kids in this photo, Sydney ran in youth AAU races.

At Faber Elementary School, fifth-grade teacher Lou DeLauro taught Sydney and her classmates to juggle. Sydney was good at it. Not only could she juggle balls and bowling pins, but she could juggle while riding a unicycle. In high school, she started a juggling club.

She continued to enter children's contests. She ran sprints, hurdles, and relay races. She also competed in the long jump. Track wasn't her only sport. In middle school, she played basketball and soccer. She also took dance lessons. But she shone brightest on the track. "All of our kids are fairly talented," her father told a reporter. "But [Sydney's] a little special. We saw [her greatness] coming. It was just a matter of time."

CHAPTER 2

TEEN PHENOM

In 2014, Sydney began her first year at Union Catholic High School in Scotch Plains, New Jersey. She joined the school track team. At her first race, she was nervous about competing against many older girls. It turned out she had nothing to fear. Not only did she win the 300-meter sprint, but she broke a New Jersey high school girl's record too.

For the next four years, Sydney won every high school hurdle event she entered. She also competed in relays and sprints and broke many school and state records. Because she was so fast, she was allowed to compete in national and international youth races. The Gatorade sports drink company gave her a high honor. It named her National Player of the Year in girl's track and field in both 2015–2016 and 2016–2017. Off the track, she had good grades and volunteered with the Central New Jersey branch of HOPE worldwide, a nonprofit organization that helps communities in need. She also volunteered with her church.

Sydney speeds ahead during a world championship event in 2015.

In July 2016, Sydney competed in her biggest event yet: the 400-meter hurdles at the US Track and Field Olympic Trials. She did well in the early heats and lined up for the final race. Her opponents were five professional runners and two college athletes. She was the only high school student in the race.

The gun sounded, and the runners took off. By the ninth hurdle, Dalilah Muhammad was in first place, with Sydney and the others fighting for the next two spots. Sydney dug in. She told herself, "I just need to push just a little bit harder." She focused on her body movements and getting over the 10th hurdle as fast as possible. Success!

McLaughlin races at the 2016 Olympic Trials.

She made it across the line in third place. She was headed to Rio de Janeiro, Brazil, for the 2016 Olympics.

Sydney turned 17 as the 2016 Olympics began. She only made it to the semifinals, but she was proud to be an Olympian. When the Olympics ended, she headed home to New Jersey to finish high school.

SUPER SPORTS SCOOP

Sydney was the youngest track-and-field athlete on the 2016 US Olympic Team. Her teammates nicknamed her Syd the Kid. But she missed the Olympics opening ceremonies because she wanted to celebrate her 17th birthday at home. Two days later, she headed to Rio.

CHAPTER 3

STAR POWER

During her last year at Union Catholic, Sydney continued to dominate on the track. Her fame began to spread. In July 2017, *Sports Illustrated* ran an article about Sydney and other national Gatorade winners. Sydney's picture was front and center on the cover of the magazine. By then she had graduated from high school and chosen to go to the University of Kentucky, which had a top track-and-field program.

At Kentucky, McLaughlin continued to win. She placed first in the women's 400-meter hurdles at the 2018 National Collegiate Athletic Association (NCAA) championships and at the 2018 Southeastern Conference (SEC) championships. She also performed well in the 4 x

McLaughlin came on strong at the 2018 NCAA championships.

400-meter relay. In this event, four teammates each run 400 meters. As one teammate finishes, they pass a baton to the next. Sydney also ran well in the 400-, 200-, and 100-meter races.

On her Instagram, Twitter, and other social media accounts, she gained thousands of followers. She was becoming a celebrity. Sportswriters wondered if she would turn pro. Pro runners can earn prize money at races. Even more money comes from endorsement deals with big companies.

McLaughlin quit college after her first year to go pro. She signed a deal with New Balance, a sports shoes and clothing company. She agreed to appear in New Balance commercials. The company created the Sydney McLaughlin Collection of running shoes and clothing.

McLaughlin speaks at a press event in 2018.

McLaughlin moved to Los Angeles to train with a new coach.

McLaughlin also teamed up with Endeavor, a company that works with many Hollywood stars and famous athletes. The company helped her get more endorsement deals. In 2018, McLaughlin moved to Los Angeles, California, to train with coach Joanna Hayes. Hayes won an Olympic gold medal in 2004.

Through all the attention, McLaughlin stayed focused. She had her sights set on her next goal: returning to the Olympics for another shot at gold.

CHAPTER 4

GOLDEN GIRL

The 2020 Olympics were planned for summer, but early in the year, the disease COVID-19 spread around the world. To protect athletes and fans from the virus, officials postponed the Summer Olympics. McLaughlin trained at a track at the University of California, Los Angeles (UCLA), but the campus shut down to keep teachers and students safe.

She kept training during the shutdown. She couldn't go to the UCLA track, so she worked out at home and ran on city streets. She enjoyed other activities, such as baking, writing poetry, and listening to music. She spent time with her boyfriend, former pro football player Andre Levrone Jr. In 2021, the two got engaged to be married.

Before the shutdown, McLaughlin trained on UCLA's track.

McLaughlin passes Felix the baton during the 4 x 400-meter relay at the 2021 Olympics.

The Olympics returned in 2021. In preparation, McLaughlin changed coaches. She began working with Bob Kersee. He also trained Allyson Felix, who had already won nine Olympic medals. Training with Kersee meant that McLaughlin and Felix practiced side by side. McLaughlin was thrilled. She had looked up to Felix since she was young.

SUPER SPORTS SCOOP

After her hurdles victory, McLaughlin ran one more Olympic race. It was the women's 4 x 400-meter relay, and it was held on her birthday. McLaughlin, Felix, Muhammad, and 800-meter gold medalist Athing Mu each ran a leg of the race. This US dream team easily took home the gold.

When summer came, McLaughlin ran her world record time at the Olympic Trials and flew to Tokyo with the US Track and Field Olympic Team. In the final 400-meter hurdles race, she stunned the world again. She passed Muhammad right before the finish line and clocked an astounding time of 51.46 seconds. She smashed her own world record and captured the gold medal.

The sports world celebrated. But McLaughlin remained cool, calm, and focused on the future. "It's just amazing to be a part of history," she told reporters who asked about her win, "to be a part of this generation that's pushing the boundaries of what's possible. And, you know, it hasn't fully hit me yet, but I do know that . . . we haven't even scratched the surface."

McLaughlin clears a hurdle during the 400-meter race. She won gold in this Olympic event.

SYDNEY McLAUGHLIN CAREER STATS

OLYMPIC MEDALS:

2

WORLD CHAMPIONSHIPS:

2

WORLD RECORDS:

1

BEST 400-METER HURDLES TIME:

51.46 SECONDS

BEST 400-METER SPRINT TIME:

50.07 SECONDS

GLOSSARY

endorsement deal: a business deal in which an athlete gets paid to use and promote a company's products

heat: a race held to see which athletes will compete at the next level

hurdles: a track event in which runners leap over barriers, called hurdles, set up on the course

nonprofit organization: a group that uses the money it makes to support a cause, such as an educational, scientific, or charitable program

Olympic Trials: an athletic contest held to determine which athletes will go to the Olympic Games

pro: short for professional, taking part in an activity to make money

relay: a team track event where each runner covers one part of a course before handing off a baton to the next runner

semifinals: the next-to-last heat in an athletic contest

sprint: a race over a short distance

SOURCE NOTES

9   James Best, "Meet Sydney McLaughlin, 400m Hurdler on the
     U.S. Olympic Track Team," NBC Los Angeles, last modified
     August 3, 2021, https://www.nbclosangeles.com/news/sports
     /tokyo-summer-olympics/meet-sydney-mclaughlin-400m
     -hurdler-on-the-u-s-olympic-track-team/2655345/.

13   "This Young Track Star Is a Generational Talent," GoodSport,
     accessed October 21, 2021, https://www.goodsport.me/this
     -young-track-star-is-a-generational-talent/.

16   "Sydney McLaughlin: HS Star to World Record Holder,"
     YouTube video, 15:31, posted by FloTrack, June 27, 2012,
     https://www.youtube.com/watch?v=omrmcxlxZK0.

27   "Sydney McLaughlin Is Just Getting Started," YouTube video,
     6:37, posted by NBC Sports, August 5, 2021, https://www
     .youtube.com/watch?v=_FEa82tLvzE.

LEARN MORE

Derr, Aaron. *Individual Sports of the Summer Games*. Egremont, MA: Red Chair, 2020.

Huddleston, Emma. *Legends of Women's Track and Field*. Mendota Heights, MN: Press Box Books, 2021.

Levit, Joe. *Track and Field's G.O.A.T: Usain Bolt, Jackie-Joyner Kersee, and More*. Minneapolis: Lerner Publications, 2022.

Sydney McLaughlin, Track and Field
https://www.teamusa.org/usa-track-and-field/athletes/sydney-mclaughlin

Track and Field
https://kids.britannica.com/kids/article/track-and-field/353870

Track and Field Athletics Facts for Kids
https://kids.kiddle.co/Track_and_field_athletics

INDEX

PHOTO ACKNOWLEDGMENTS

Image credits: Ashley Landis/AP/Shutterstock.com, p. 4; Andy Lyons/
Getty Images, pp. 6, 8–9; Patrick Smith/Getty Images, pp. 7, 15–16; Quinn
Rooney/Getty Images, p. 10; AP Photo/Charlie Neibergall, p. 11; Bob
Daemmrich/Alamy Stock Photo, p. 12; Paul Gilham/Getty Images, p. 14;
AP Photo/Chris Pizzello, p. 18; AP Photo/Phelan M. Ebenhack, p. 19; AP
Photo/Kirby Lee, p. 21; Barry Winiker/Getty Images, p. 22; Cameron
Spencer/Getty Images, p. 23; Al Seib/Los Angeles Times/Getty Images,
p. 24; Ryan Pierse/Getty Images, p. 25; Kyodo News/Getty Images, p. 27.
Design elements: Tamjaii9/Shutterstock.com; The Hornbills Studio/
Shutterstock.com.

Cover: Chine Nouvelle/SIPA/Shutterstock.com.